The Rest of Love

ALSO BY CARL PHILLIPS

POETRY

In the Blood

Cortège

From the Devotions

Pastoral

The Tether

Rock Harbor

PROSE

Coin of the Realm: Essays on the Life and Art of Poetry

TRANSLATION

Sophocles: Philoctetes

CARL PHILLIPS

The Rest of Love

Farrar, Straus and Giroux

NEW YORK

Farrar, Straus and Giroux
19 Union Square West, New York 10003

Grateful acknowledgment is made to the editors of the following journals, in which these poems appeared:

Boston Review: "Like Cuttings for a Wreath of Praise and Ransom," "Mastery"; *Callaloo*: "North"; *Five Fingers Review*: "Vow"; *Fourteen Hills*: "Anthem," "Conduct"; *Hotel Amerika*: "Aubade: Some Peaches, After Storm," "If a Wilderness," "Late, in a Time of Splendor"; *Kenyon Review*: "Here, on Earth," "Hymns and Fragments," "Like Stitches Where the Moths Have Made an Opening"; *Kestrel*: "Crew"; *Michigan Quarterly Review*: "Fray"; *The Nation*: "Custom," "The Rest of Love"; *New England Review*: "Fervor"; *The New Yorker*: "White Dog"; *Pequod*: "The Grackle," "Sunset, with Severed Head of Orpheus"; *Pool*: "Singing," "Sudden Scattering of Leaves, All Gold"; *Salmagundi*: "All It Takes," "In Love," "Late Apollo," "The Rescue"; *Tin House*: "Pleasure"; *TriQuarterly*: "In Stone," "Sanctum," "Tower Window," "Trophy," "The Way As Promised"; "Fresco: Cove and Spur" was commissioned by the Getty Research Institute as part of a program centered on the theme "Reproductions and Originals."

Library of Congress Cataloging-in-Publication Data
Phillips, Carl, 1959–
    The rest of love / Carl Phillips.— 1st ed.
      p. cm.
    ISBN 0-374-24953-9 (alk. paper)
    I. Title

PS3566.H476R47 2003
811'.54— dc21

             2003045213

Designed by Jonathan D. Lippincott

www.fsgbooks.com

10 9 8 7 6 5 4 3 2 1

For Doug

Contents

The Rest of Love

And it was clear to both of them that the end was still far, far off, and that the most complicated and difficult part was just beginning.

—Anton Chekhov

Sanctum

CUSTOM

There is a difference it used to make,
seeing three swans in this versus four in that
quadrant of sky. I am not imagining. It was very large, as its
effects were. Declarations of war, the timing fixed upon for a sea-
      departure; or,
about love, a sudden decision not to, to pretend instead to a kind
of choice. It was dramatic, as it should be. Without drama,
what is ritual? I look for omens everywhere, because they are everywhere
to be found. They come to me like strays, like the damaged,
something that could know better, and should, therefore—but does not:
a form of faith, you've said. I call it sacrifice—an instinct for it, or a habit
      at first, that
becomes required, the way art can become, eventually, all we have
of what was true. You shouldn't look at me like that. Like one of those
      saints
on whom the birds once settled freely.

TOWER WINDOW

The glass is old:
through it, the world—
its parts—
coming up:
is it spring then?

To look through it,
I could be looking through
river-water, the river
slowing but
never down, quite, to
stillness—

I had thought so,
I had wanted to think so.
Was that wrong, then?

Last night, the storm was
hours approaching.
Too far, still, to be heard.
Only the sky, when lit—
less flashing than
quivering brokenly

(a wing,
not any wing,
a sparrow's)—for a sign.

It seemed exactly the way
I've loved you.

And you a stone,
marked *Gone Already*—
you
a leaf,
marked *Spattered Milk*

in that light, then out of.

I closed my eyes. I
dreamed again the dream
called *Yes: the worst
is true.*
In it,
I wake.
I lean my head against the glass.
How cool the glass is.

LATE, IN A TIME OF SPLENDOR

All day, I've watched it, the blue
hydrangea's tossing shadow. The only pattern is
that it changes; routinely, what was—
gets lost.
There was one whose eyes, from
certain angles, seemed
different depths of the same
mistake. Another who, during sex, would shout
The will of God, as if brandishing
a flag whose meaning—consolation,
triumph—I never required.
As when to believe in a thing
can be, and
then must become, enough. What if,
about desire, it won't have mattered
how I saw it—lifting, like a body
not yet steady from that first
unsteadying break
in dream: for a moment, all bells ring true.

TROPHY

I.
When was the burning
that of fire?

When was it fear?

When sorrow?

That any gesture can be understood
as the necessary, mostly incidental
price the body pays
for whatever response comes

past gesture,

past the body that made it:

to what extent can this be said, and
it be true? and
it be false?
Under what conditions?

Under whose conditions?

Thus the waves.
Thus the light of the sun
across them.

II.
Above me, what before had seemed
entirely that to which my own passage—swift,
coracled, resplendent, over
the water—might stand compared

are clouds now,

now interruption,

the way that water is interruption,
the land only ending
apparently,

there, where not so long ago
I pushed off from it,

it does not end . . .

It seems I am rowing,

it seems
to the rhythm of
a song there's nothing
left of

except the rhythm,

no notes,

a broken line, the words, to
—guessing—sing to, *No,* sing
No, I'll have no other—

      Say what you will.

      Say all you have to.

I have looked to the water:
there it was, of course, doing
the water's version of pucker, then
bloom,
then sprawl.

I look to the shore as if
toward everything that, once,
I stood for, and—
how soon, already—

almost, I cannot see it, I

look to the water,

I am rowing, it seems

SINGING

Overheard,
late, this morning: *Don't blame
me, if I am everything your heart
has led to.*

Hazel trees;
ghost-moths in the hazel branches.
Why not stay?

It's a dream I've had
twice now: God is real, as
the difference between
having squandered faith and having lost it
is real. He's straightforward:

when he says *Look at me when I'm speaking*,
it means he's speaking.
He's not unreasonable:

because I've asked, he shows me his mercy—
a complicated arrangement
of holes and

hooks, buckles. *What else did you think
mercy looked like,*

he says and, demonstrating, he straps it on, then takes it off.

THE REST OF LOVE

The hive is for where
the honey was.
Was findable there,

then not.
Sometimes, I think I dreamed it,
or I am saying it like a thing

that I would do,
when I would never,
and calling it art:

that first time;
that second time . . .
That's how it starts—

I know as much about mythology
as, by now,
you must also. The bull

for slaughter; the number of days
required for the carcass to rot
correctly—

so that eventually, the bees come back,
lifting the dropped veil of
themselves up,

into the air, like some
dark and obvious
exception to a rule

I once knew. Is it true that
nothing lacks, given
the right comparison,

its charm?
In the story,
it is difficult to say

whether Orpheus is stupid,
or is heartless, or—what,
human?

He looks back.
He's lost everything.

And his own story begins in earnest.

VOW

Unpatterned rustling,
the kinds of trees—pine,
scrub oak—you'll have
seen before.

Is it latchless, or only
unlatched,
that door,
slamming?

By *disarray*,
I mean the look findable
in the eyes of a horse in storm,
and panicking.

What I mean by *luster:*
look,
see the black of its mane?

Thunder,
a lasso coming close, that
just misses.

Manured hay bales;
dirt the damp has kept,
days now,
from traveling far.

As far as conquest?
No. Not that far.

As far as the urge to
rise and begin conquering? No,

farther.
Incongruities.
Tiger lilies—
little slaves, little

slaves in the light—
as an example. Words
to a childhood song
I'd thought forgotten, but

parts come back. I lie down.
I wear nothing at all.

LIKE STITCHES WHERE THE MOTHS
HAVE MADE AN OPENING

Star-in-the-hand   Cupped fire   Fist,
luminous.
          What keeps staying lost is not,
anymore, the thing itself, but the definition
it once provided,
                    as history does to what
occurs—to what has not, yet.
                              Leafe-gold, what is
blown—is blowable—*away.*
                    God enters me
as if from behind; he shakes, inside me. *I want*
what you want, he says. I say *Why regard what I*
can't choose? To be anchorless,
                              but not unanchored:
To have failed means, at worst, once we flourished,
that's right, isn't it?
                    Windfall whose imperfections
fade in a shabby harvest, the body—as again from
mistakes all the same enjoyed—lifts, staggers,
like light
          off spokes of a wheel set spinning,
                                        as the wheel
slows down: speed of legend, of the myth that follows,
of the life that a myth eclipses. Speed of
                              Don't.
Not now. Listen: someone is calling my name.

LATE APOLLO

I.
Brief in the light of streetlamp, then back again,
into dark—two boys, throwing a ball between them.
The younger one is almost handsome, a star
already, going down.
                        At last the snow lies
unoracular,

unstepped across.
                        If I could speak, I'd speak
to no one, now. I'd remember the way everyone
else does: later, when none of it matters,
memory as good as a mirror for changing things,
no good at all:

                        You're in a garden,
you've trellised the dwarf cherry, trained it so as,
branching, to become—and cast in shadow against the wall—
this fan, opening, held open, the way a map is held
in wind—

            The map makes the getting there
at first look easy: a prairie, then the mountains, then the sea.

II.
And now it is as we wanted it.
And now they are very still:

the grapes, rampant once;
                          the roses that—
like grace—require no training
to swag and scramble;
                          the waters there . . .

A stillness like that of music resting—or sex,
after: what they call sadness, though it
is not sadness.

                 Country to which, increasingly, I've
felt native. I believe
I could—

                 Like asking at first *Where am I*
after dream—and the room, in pieces, slow,
comes back:
                 a language that, all this time, we knew.

Here comes the word for mystery.
Here is the word for true.

III.
As if everything were in the effect, finally.
Less the wind itself, than a quickness,
or lack of it, with which the gulls, lifting,

move forward; or how the trees, here at
shoreline, recall or don't the startled angle
of retreat-before-temptation that is fixed,

apparently, instinctive in the saint—this is
how, in the old, illuminated paintings,
the saints most easily can be picked out

from the crowd around them, the crowd
whose purpose, I think, must be to remind us
that the world is larger, will always be larger

than its exceptions. The crowd equals
what's forgettable. The light, for as far as
I can see, is that of any number of late

afternoons I remember still: how the light
seemed a bell; how it seemed I'd been living
inside it, waiting— I'd heard all about

that one clear note it gives.

MASTERY

Dry waterfall

              that eventually, almost,
the skull resembled—

And then the skull was just

a skull.
        The heart—
at last nothing

but a muscle moving,

not at all the talisman you'd imagined:
how if only you could touch it—how
everything, everything might

yet be different
if you did . . .
           Is this
perfection,

        or the cost of it?

If the mind seems

increasingly a landscape
where brush and desert, dry
prairie, and chaparral
coincide,

              is this that landscape,
or the abandoned
set, finally, for one of those movies

that take place there: sudden

sandstorm, each man
immediately dismounting, each blinding,
with whatever cloth available,

his horse's eyes . . .

              That much, still,
is true, isn't it?—the horse

comes first? then you do?

ALL IT TAKES

Any force—
generosity, sudden updraft.
Fear. Things invisible,

and the visible effects by which
we know them. Human gesture. Betrayed,
betrayed. The dampness of fog as

understandable by how, inside it, from within their
thicket of nowhere left to hide—
that leafless—the winter berries, more than usual,

shine. First always
comes the ability to believe, and then the need to.
The ancient Greeks; the Romans after. How they

made of love a wild god; of fidelity—a small,
a tame one. I am no less grateful for
the berries than for the thorns that are

meant, I think, to help. As if
sometimes the world really did amount to
a quiet arrangement. Cut flowers. Make

death the one whose eyes are lidless. And
—already—you are leaving. You have
crossed the water.

The Way As Promised

IN STONE

Their clothes; their rings as well, until
at last they wore nothing. All was visible:
flourish; humiliation; some things,
more than others, looking almost the same.
As if *Not only torn but lavish let be*
the angle all tearing starts at,
as if this were the rule, each
splitting open around, unfolding
from—so as, incidentally, to expose—
its wet center. The kind of sweetness that
carries a room, but there
was no room. How at first a sweetness;
how, by turns, a gift, a darkness.
Very dark, especially, about the trees, where
trees were. Like being a child and told, all
over again, *Think of Christ as of a pilot boat,*
a launch delayed slightly, but reliable,
it will come— There, beside the shifting fact of
all that water. What's done is done.

CONDUCT

Here—
your shirt, he said,
after. Lifting it. Bringing it

to me as if it were
not a shirt
but a thing immaculate,

or in flames, or—
with a single sword
positioned through it—

a sacred heart.
Handling it
like a woman shown

handling laundry in a wind
between two wars while,
in the distance,

shadow-like,
migrants work the fields'
abundance,

drift—like wind,
like war—to the next
farm, the next,

as to a lover, as far into
fall as whenever the cold stops
the need to do so,

the way that truth, when
it is brutal—though no less
beautiful for

being brutal
than for being true—can at first
stop everything except

an instinct
to get more close, take it:
gift, ransom— How turn away? How

not rush forward,
and fold it—in flames, immaculate—
in your arms?

WHITE DOG

First snow—I release her into it—
I know, released, she won't come back.
This is different from letting what,

already, we count as lost go. It is nothing
like that. Also, it is not like wanting to learn what
losing a thing we love feels like. Oh yes:

I love her.
Released, she seems for a moment as if
some part of me that, almost,

I wouldn't mind
understanding better, is that
not love? She seems a part of me,

and then she seems entirely like what she is:
a white dog,
less white suddenly, against the snow,

who won't come back. I know that; and, knowing it,
I release her. It's as if I release her
because I know.

FERVOR

Somewhere between
To Be Lit
and To Be

Transfigured,
he'd removed his shirt,
his shoes,

he had opened his pants;
he wore nothing under.

I did what I do—

pretended to be a fallen gate,
its hinges gone, that
soon the snow,

continuing, must hide
most of.

Is this how it will finish?
Is fervor belief's
only measure? Is there

no saving
what betrays itself?

After which,
I held him
until his body was not

his body,
was a single birch
I'd seen years ago—

down, and silvering
in a field,

Indiana.

Sleep, I said. But he
couldn't sleep;
he said *Tell me a story.*

*There was once
a mockingbird,* I told him, *It
knew no better:*

it would sing.

It sang all night . . .

IN LOVE

Here, when the light deepens,

when they say
The dark is taking hold,

and mean a gradualness
like that of discipline where,
once, abandon figured,

the men who—all day, a month now—
have worked the orchard
leave the orchard behind;

they have left already.
Some of them rub olive oil
into their hands: they believe

a well-oiled hand aches less—
and that is true.
One of these hands, tomorrow,

will be the first one
pointed at the boy who, by
now, is finished—

he must be:
isn't it his, the body that hangs there,
the body whose stillness is

the same, isn't it,
as the leaves in stillness? As if
there were no distinction:

the leaves,
the body;
this boy, and

any boy mistaking always
the smell of hay,
shit, and harness

for the smell of horses. That
is another story.
In my own,

I want a whip;
I want a pistol. And the Lord,

being good, provides.

THE RESCUE

But the field he brings me to, it is
a winter field, colorless, reduced to a stubble
he calls deliberate. If it must

come to fields, and stubble, then what do
I know?
Maybe the tree from which the pods hang—flat,

like snap peas—is the black locust
that he says it is,
and not the honey locust, named

for how its pods—not flat, but twisted—
contain a sweetness
so sweet, he says, the cattle recognize it, will

cross the field for it. It could be true. But
the water seems just as likely—the river that, from here,
keeps changing: first a river,

then the ceaseless muscle-work
of a history bright
and dark,

then a broidered shirt—
silk, discarded
for how it flattereth the king no more—

then again a river.
Why does it seem
I won't come back here? Why speak of it

as of, already, a place I miss?
Slow, familiar,
he says *Look at the light where it hits*

the water. He points to it
as if to something more
difficult than this

to see. What I see is the light falling
all around us.
It falls like decline on a living legend's perfect face.

SUDDEN SCATTERING OF LEAVES, ALL GOLD

Sir,
the flies assemble
like so many parts of a working argument
around what proves it. No sign, not yet,
of the rains you spoke of. —Will they come,
ever?
        It's day, mostly. The light
extends like truth, the truth like
a hand extending at the same time as
it recedes.
            What is *that* like?
One moment, I'm a pitcher of
milk tipped dangerously forward; the next,
a band of pilgrims, pilgriming
toward the latest report: pieces of heaven again—
here, on earth.
                Between tenderness
and violent force, if the choice is easy,
why then does each seem equally, with the same
persuasiveness, a form of luck
beneath which—
                beneath which, I
should know better?
                    In the meadow, in
adoration: am I not yours?

THE WAY AS PROMISED
(Santiago de Compostela)

He shot the ass
in the head. Simple.
He filled the hole between

its eyes, open, with a spray
of indigo—
for blue, he said,

for yellow, sweetleaf—and
all was green: the bush clover
soon to be translated

into hay,
the blades of the willow
beneath which he told us

*Technically, the weight of pain
is the weight of shadow*
and it was true. It was

as he'd said: we passed
protected. Here's where our mounts,
thirsting, took of the water,

fell swiftly dead, and thereby
saved us. Here's where we
stopped to bathe, and

for the first time
saw him naked—
one tattoo: a deer, gutted,

pinned in what he called
your standard
Christ-on-the-cross position,

by which, it seems now, he meant in
no way a thing
unholy.

•

      Here he is, taking my hand—
first to his chest,
then his mouth,

saying, as if toward someone who
has not read as much already, *This road*
goes far.

      And here—
past that—saying
Listen,

what makes the truth so difficult
is also what
draws us to it: how clear it is.

•

A single road.

      As far as Santiago.

NORTH

Earthstar,
seastar—
more dark than either—he mistakes me.

Lies beneath me.
Has arched already himself up in
such a way.

He is
—what? an instance of glory
outglorying the bearer of it?
Token when it conquers
that for which it stood?

Those who give without receipt,
without even the expectation of receipt—
I am not among them.

As if having spoken, and
now could watch the words find, spatter-like, his chest,
a brightness that
depends finally,
any shield,

—a wall across which, random, off of water, light
shifts,
reflected.

What if the will
were husk entirely,
and the husk,
breakable,
were broken open, to
where the seeds are? what
then? what would the seeds
be?

A cathedral, falling.

One of those doves that, in the Greek original, the sufferer's bow
brings down.

O him, beneath me.

HYMNS AND FRAGMENTS

These are the gloves—of doeskin—he had specially made,
after, and never wore.

He'd shot the animal himself—
unfairly, it seemed at the time; still seems so: crouched
in a locust tree,

bow-and-arrow. There had been, he said,
no struggle . . . Of his own dying,

he said it was like
many things, but mostly like watching a harbor slowly
empty of the ships it held,

the one that brought him here
leaving among them, distinguished

easily by its single
low-masted sail that—raised, risen—seems a sail
no longer but, more,

a shield from which all device, all
signature of heraldry has been cleared

as a mark of
expulsion from what turns out to have been, at
best, a ragged nobility—

what's to regret? Naked that
first time I ever saw him,

                    naked now: in this light,
he looks—his body looks—like a set of instructions I
don't expect

            I'll need. Here's how to keep what's good
from spoiling—

            This is how you paint a sleeping bird.

FRESCO: COVE AND SPUR

The stone rises, with its runes, from the sea.

If I remember it, did it happen?

Part horse,
part man, dragging
away by the hair
the bride who, alone in the scene, lifts
no cry.

      Here, as token of thanks for
how the withered limb was made
strong again,

how the infant swam miraculously
free of the raft
of blindness,

each has left his particular
mark, that the stone
carries easily,
each as weightless
as a scar
is weightless,

if nobody stares, is it
gone?
Is it?

Graffito—

Tattoo,

      what changes as the flesh it
adorns changes, until
the image itself
has grown distorted past
all recognition save
that of memory: here, once,

was the reveler—
cap-and-bells,

beads; here, the stitcher of leather
into release, restraint,
costume; and here,

part horse, part man,
fallen already, having
shoved already his way
up, from behind,
into and—

and into—.

Familiar light

The stone

The sea

As when all photographs
prove nothing.

                    I have known a man
to rouse from within
the wind-rifled field of
long fever,

he'll rise,

he'll take eagerly
the cool water, he appears,
at first, most restored . . .

The Rest of Love

IF A WILDERNESS

Then spring came:
                    branches-in-a-wind . . .

I bought a harness, I bought a bridle.
I wagered on God in a kind stranger—
kind at first; strange, then less so—
and I was right.
                    The difference between
God and luck is that luck, when it leaves,
does not go far: the idea is to believe
you could almost touch it . . .

                                Now he's
singing, cadence of a rough sea— A way of
crossing a dark so unspecific, it seems
everywhere: isn't that what singing, once,
was for?
              I lay the harness across my lap,
the bridle beside me for the sweat—the color
and smell of it—that I couldn't, by now,
lift the leather free of, even if I wanted to.

I don't want to.

SUNSET, WITH SEVERED HEAD OF ORPHEUS

He spoke of the sea
as of something offered up and then
unto the light,

as if example: *how
for every image,
there's the rest of the world, where*

*everything but, it seems,
that image turns,
contained.*

We lay on the shore.
We looked out at the sea. Plovers,
yes. Gulls. Horizon.

But the sea was itself,
not watered silk.
And the clearness of the water

was not the clarity with which
I've known, always,
that the capacity for

love does not increase but is
fixed in each of us,
a corridor whose

dark length
discourages at
first our going

down it, or
very far.
Then we go farther . . .

One vastness
is not the next one.
How it may seem—was that ever

the point? Here is the distance
between what he has
said to me and

all that I understand.
And here, dividing
what I tell him from what I don't:

yet another.
Where we lie
on the shore. We look out at the sea.

AUBADE: SOME PEACHES,
AFTER STORM

So that each
is its own, now—each a fallen, blond stillness.
Closer, above them,
the damselflies pass as they would over water,
if the fruit were water,
or as bees would, if they weren't
somewhere else, had the fruit found
already a point more steep
in rot, as soon it must, if
none shall lift it from the grass whose damp only
softens further those parts where flesh
goes soft.

There are those
whom no amount of patience looks likely
to improve ever, I always said, meaning
gift is random,
assigned here,
here withheld—almost always
correctly,
as it's turned out: how your hands clear
easily the wreckage;
how you stand—like a building for a time condemned,
then deemed historic. Yes. You
will be saved.

THE GRACKLE

Where tree line's highest leaves meet
and end
is canopy—reason

why not all of the light descends
as entirely as now
the grackle does,

yet another variation
(as if the lesson
could not be taught

too often,
and example the one way left) on
how it must be,

to be distractible
only by what is
immediate to—

and knowable by—
the senses,
whatever senses at least

the grackle
this long has lived by and
now, descending,

not asking
Is it
indifference,

not asking
How can it be that Christ is as
everywhere

unapparently
as they have said, has
reached the ground,

has stepped across the tree-shadowed
part of it, will
any moment enter the very

light to which
what will the bird most
be, then, if not the blue and

bronze and black and verdigris exception—

PLEASURE

This far in—
where to say *the sea*
and mean *impossible*

makes sense,
why not—you can
almost forget

what brought you here,
the water it started with,
a life that has sometimes (admit

this much) seemed mostly
an only half-wanted because
finally unruly

animal you'd once hoped
to change by changing
its name: from *If Only* to

How Did I
to *In Spite of Everything*—
but nothing sticks, that doesn't

have to. Not memory;
not the naming—which, if a form of
remembering, is also

a form of *to own*, possession,
whose lineage
shifts never: traced

far enough, past hope, back across
belief, it ends always
at desire—without which

would there have been
imagination, would
there be folly,

one spreading itself
like a bay tree, the other
a green olive tree in the house

of God?
This far in, sky
is everything. Clouds cross it

like ships,
sheer will, regret
itself cut abruptly

loose. Lovely, when you say so,
—and when you don't.
It was never for you.

HERE, ON EARTH

I.
When the battle, like favor, shifts
in Greek epic, there are smaller signs inside
the large ones:
                    an otherwise random soldier,
around whom none of the story apparently
figures, has removed

                    his headgear, its horsehair plume
stirs barely, and it is fate
and a breeze only, *Never again* and *Sure,*
                              why not—

both, and neither.
                    Everything,
as always in epic, has changed forever.

Moth, consuming what is dearest to it— There
is a glamour,
              even to a thing undoing itself,
there is— Sing it:

One of them was sucking the others—in turn, slowish—off.

A kiss where roughly, in the dark, his brow should be.

II.
If out of the distance between descent
                              and the memory of it
could be spun a thread,
I'd make a softness,
                    I'd be the tortoiseshell boat
wrapped soft

          inside it, where nothing shines.

That was yesterday. There's little
that won't sound reasonable
                          for a time. Then reason passes,

the speed of traveling
                      stays constant,
we have merely become, ourselves,
                              more conscious of it.

Only days ago, the peonies opened—and already—
Just look at them: group portrait

of a winter river the thaw
                          has touched,
and now takes hold of—and soon must possess entirely.

III.
As if I were afraid, as if I should be, as after
a series of blows
                    staggered back from in a wind

all crash and spray, like struck
water, and the wind had spoken:
"The body as hieroglyph for silence"—what does

that mean? and
                    What if discretion is
not a blade—dropped, retrieved—that we drop again?

Radiance unrelenting—
no peace, no shadow,
no shelter now—

                    I clap my hands
over all of it: *What's ruined?*
                              What isn't yet?

I clap my hands: A field, and as if I'd fallen here before,
and I'd forgotten.
                    That's not possible—

You carried me. You took me. You hid your face.

ANTHEM

Trapped bee at the glass.

A window.

Instinct is different from
to understand.

Is not the same.

The window is not the light
it fills with—has
been filling with—

What the bee ascends to.

Is full with.

To ascend.
To have been foiled.
To be consistent.

Instinct making
its own equations.

The window is not, for the bee, a window.

Is a form of resistance

not understood
because not understandable,
not in terms

of reason.
A felt force.

A force entirely:

And I said Yes. That it
had been

like that. Resistance
equaling,
at first, the light— And then resistance

as only one of the light's more difficult

and defining features.

LIKE CUTTINGS FOR A WREATH OF PRAISE AND RANSOM

Abbreviation,
                    part that gives what is left
away. As if released,
                    a stone—as from
a sling. The landscape opening as if no end to it,
a longing anywhere
                    for some resistance, some
stop: the magnolia, its ring of bird-ravaged
seed-cones,
                    the birds themselves, a wind lifting
a collar of feathers at the neck of each—stiff
courtiers,
           Elizabethan. Clarity, versus
blur.
     Fine distinctions.
                    Not, it seems,
the cries of joy. Not punishment—think
in terms of, instead,
                    persuasion. Silo, through which
the rains, passing,
                    pass unimpeded. Hunger,
versus the pursuit of it. That's what they say.
With time, with wear,
                    the leather softening. They say
the legs go here. The straps adjust.
                              Like so.

SANCTUM

Then broke off reading.

Then closed his book.

Systematic,
erotic,
not unreluctant,

half-shedding earlier versions of itself undone,
undoing—was

that the body, no different
finally from the light as
he'd grown tired of seeing it

over, over again,
depicted?

Hovering.

Nakedness, it had always been
translatable: "what lacks assistance"

—how had he not noticed?

Deceit, trespass,
whether risked or actual:
as boring at last as

the kind of gesture that
looks each time like, for its
flourish, *Here it ends, it must,* when

—does it?

A coffered ceiling—

A single window, round, leaded and,

viewable from it, the usual horses, black,
caparisoned, across their backs the stiff
marriage of brocade
and a velvet

crimped,
crumpled,
to heraldic effect—

Why not? he said.

Why can't I? he said.

Twin bells, those questions,
seeming,

ringing as from a bracelet at the wrist that had
worn no bracelet.

He moved at first,
as if deliberately,
in concert with what he believed

might least offend. And only then as if
for flight.

FRAY

There it lay, before me, as they had
said it would: a distance
I'd wish to cross,

then try to, then leave
off wishing. Words like *arc,*
and *trajectory.* And *push.* The words

themselves over time
coming to matter
the way, in painting, color does: less,

finally, than the gesture
each stroke
memorializes.

A kind of sleep
that will look like death,
they said,

A kind of waking that will look
bewildered.
I woke,

as it were. I was not
bewildered. The distance as uncrossed
as it had been,

but now a clarity—like that
of vision. A kind of crossing.
Parts that the light

reached, relative
to everything else, what the light
kept missing. Spirea

in a wind; wind in the spirea's
leggy branches—I could make
distinctions: weeping

spruce; weeping maple. I could love you
as I had loved you—as only
humans can love each other: it's

a human need,
to give to shapelessness
a form.

CREW
(St. John's)

Most wore shirts—oversized,
shabby-aquarium-green
singlets that the light

off the water at once
filled, making
the bodies inside

visible: their lack
of fullness, what
eventually they would come

into, briefly
the body seemed what it
never is

—ignorable,
a small concern.

But the boy at the bow was shirtless:

how bells at evensong,
though this was morning, leave
changed the air—

Facing the others, he watched them
pull in unison their
course across and

over again the water,
as if to the rowing there were now
no struggling,

or it was as if—about struggling—
the only difficult part left
lay in settling

finally on a pattern for it.
Three strokes; four—

And the boy at the bow sang out to them:

What is dread
but that from which the soul
will be delivered?

        To which *O what*
is the soul? the rest of the boys
sang back.

Notes

The epigraph to the book is the final sentence in Chekhov's story "The Lady with the Little Dog," in *Anton Chekhov: Stories* (Richard Pevear and Larissa Volokhonsky, trans.), Bantam Books, 2000.

"Tower Window"

The comparison of lightning to a broken wing—specifically, a sparrow's—is drawn loosely from Turgenev's description of "what the peasants call a Sparrow Night" on page 48 of his novella *First Love*, Isaiah Berlin (trans.), Penguin, 1982.

"Like Stitches Where the Moths Have Made an Opening"

The italics are from a sermon preached April/June 1623 by John Donne. See *John Donne: Selected Prose*, Neil Rhodes (ed.), Penguin, 1987.

"The Way As Promised"

The last two lines are fragments of the sentence " . . . thence a single road leads as far as Santiago," from chapter 1 of *The Pilgrim's Guide to Santiago de Compostela*, William Melczer (trans.), Italica Press, 1993.

"North"

The Greek original referred to is Sophocles' *Philoctetes*, whose hero by the same name has only his bow and arrow with which to secure food—doves included.

"Hymns and Fragments"

The last line paraphrases a heading from *The Mustard Seed Garden Manual of Painting*, Mai-mai Sze (ed. and trans.), Princeton University Press, 1978.

"Fresco: Cove and Spur"

The first two lines are my translation of the first line of Edwin Morgan's Scots translation of Heinrich Heine's poem "Es Ragt ins Meer der Runenstein." Morgan's translation appears in his *Collected Translations*, Carcanet, 1996. The image of the seemingly restored but in fact still direly ill man is used by Cicero to describe the state of the Roman Republic in the peroration of his speech *In Catilinam, I.*

"Pleasure"

For the images of a spreading bay tree and of a green olive tree in the house of God, see Psalms 37 and 52, respectively.

"Here, on Earth"

"Moth, consuming what is dearest to it": see Psalm 39.

"*The body as hieroglyph for silence*": the phrasing both arises from and is in response to Donne's line "The *Hieroglyphique* of silence, is the hand upon the mouth" (italics his) from a sermon preached probably 11 February 1627. See *John Donne: Selected Prose*, Neil Rhodes (ed.), Penguin, 1987.

Of discretion as a blade (with which to smite down temptation daily), see chapter 33 of *The Cloud of Unknowing*, Clifton Wolters (trans.), Penguin, 1961.